Jake's Bones

Jake McGowan-Lowe

Consultant: Paolo Viscardi

Ticktock

A big thank you to Mum and Dad, Paolo Viscardi, Ben Garrod,
Mrs Powell, Ric Morris, Mr Evans, Catherine Smith, Ben Williams,
Chris Packham, Professor Black and Lucina at CAHID, Michael Fox,
Sarah Potten and all the other adults who helped and inspired
and encouraged me with my bone collection.

Jake McGowan-Lowe,
Scotland 2014

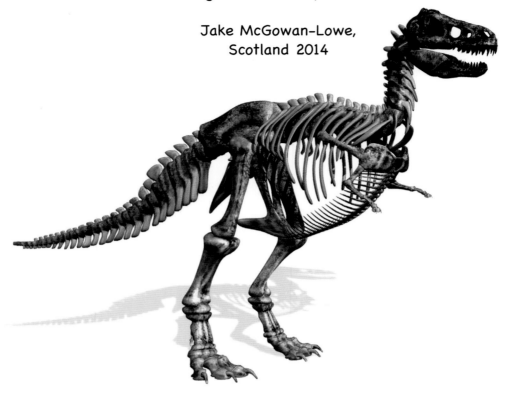

An Hachette UK Company
www.hachette.co.uk

First published in Great Britain in 2014 by Ticktock,
an imprint of Octopus Publishing Group Ltd
Endeavour House
189 Shaftesbury Avenue
London
WC2H 8JY
www.octopusbooks.co.uk
www.ticktockbooks.co.uk

ISBN 978 1 78325 025 7

A CIP record for this book is available from the British Library.

Printed and bound in China

1 3 5 7 9 10 8 6 4 2

 Project Editor and additional material by Joanne Bourne   Design: Ian Butterworth
Illustrator: Fabio Santomauro   Publisher: Tim Cook   Art Director: Ellie Wahba
Managing Editor: Karen Rigden   Senior Production Manager: Peter Hunt
Picture Manager: Jennifer Veall   With thanks to Keira Stuart-Smith
Additional photoshop: John Lingham

Contents

This is me with a cow skull.

My name is Jake and I collect bones . . .

I live in a small village with my mum, my dad, my baby brothers Sam and Harry and my two cats.

I love walking, exploring, watching wildlife and collecting bones. I've been collecting bones since I was six, and I started my blog about bones when I was seven.

www.jakes-bones.com

And this is me with a cat skull.

This book is all about the bones I have collected. There are also lots of incredible facts about other amazing bones from around the world.

Look! This is a whale's skeleton.

This is a monkey skull.

I have more than 200 skulls on display in my bedroom. Mostly I find them when I'm out on my walks. I've also been sent lots of skulls by people all over the world. I've got a seal, puffins, seabirds and even monkeys!

You can learn a lot about animals from their bones, from what kind of animal it is to how old it was, plus how it adapted to where it lived!

This is a sheep. Look at the square molar teeth for grinding grass.

I give my skeletons names so I know which one is which. I named this sheep Montferno.

This is a leopard. Its pointy teeth are for hunting and fighting.

Come with me on an amazing journey and discover the real inside story of the animal world.

5

What are bones?

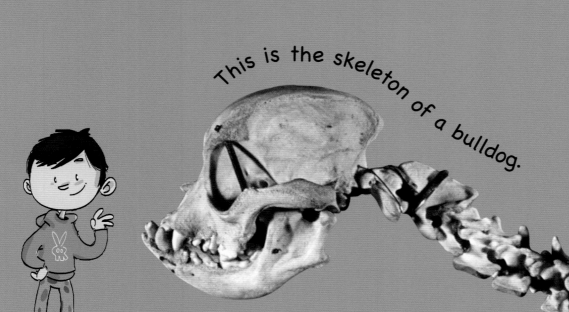

This is the skeleton of a bulldog.

Bones give humans and other animals their shape. They are a frame for their bodies. While humans and animals are alive, their bones are alive too, and have very important jobs to do.

Bones need to be strong, and they need to be light. They are made of lots of different things including calcium salts and collagen. Some bits are organic, which means they are alive, and some bits are inorganic, which means they are a bit like rock.

On the outside they are smooth. This bit is called compact bone. But on the inside bones have many layers that look a bit like a sponge. This sponge-like structure helps to keep bones light, and protects the bone marrow on the inside – a jelly-like substance that makes blood cells.

Animal Fact

Bulldogs have an unusual lower jaw which sticks out because humans have bred them to look that way.

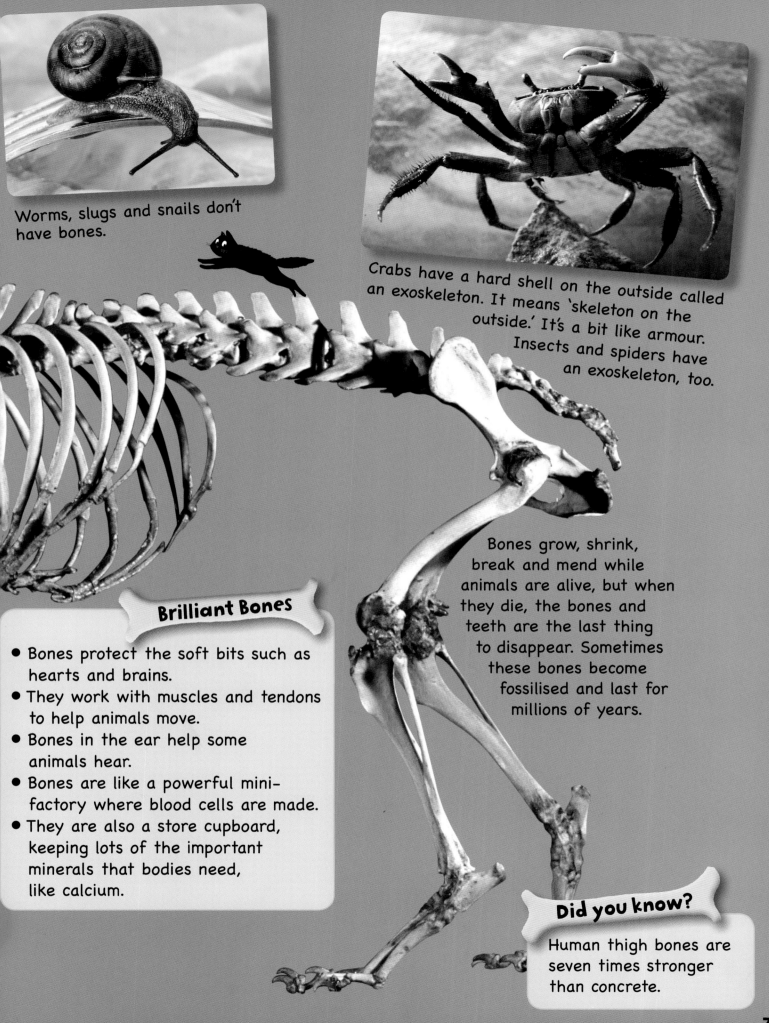

Worms, slugs and snails don't have bones.

Crabs have a hard shell on the outside called an exoskeleton. It means 'skeleton on the outside.' It's a bit like armour. Insects and spiders have an exoskeleton, too.

Bones grow, shrink, break and mend while animals are alive, but when they die, the bones and teeth are the last thing to disappear. Sometimes these bones become fossilised and last for millions of years.

Brilliant Bones

- Bones protect the soft bits such as hearts and brains.
- They work with muscles and tendons to help animals move.
- Bones in the ear help some animals hear.
- Bones are like a powerful mini-factory where blood cells are made.
- They are also a store cupboard, keeping lots of the important minerals that bodies need, like calcium.

Did you know?

Human thigh bones are seven times stronger than concrete.

Is it a bone?

I find animal bones all over the place when I'm out on walks in woods, fields and on beaches. Sometimes the bones are all together in a skeleton, which makes them easy to identify, but sometimes the bones are on their own. **So how do you know if you've found a bone?**

*turn to pages 12-13 to find out.

Shape
Bones come in all shapes and sizes and can look quite strange! Take a look at some of the amazing bones in this book. Can you guess what these bones are?*

Colour
Bones can be lots of different colours, depending on how old they are and what has happened to them.

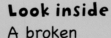

Look inside
A broken bone will sometimes look spongy on the inside, like this.

Most bones you find are a dirty white colour, but sometimes they are yellow, grey, dark brown or even green.

8

There are all sorts of things that aren't bones from the main skeleton, but they're just as interesting!

Horns

Horns can be curly and knobbly or smooth and quite straight. They are often made of tough stuff called keratin (the same as your hair and fingernails) and are hollow with a bony core inside that grows out of the skull.

This is a mouflon, an old type of sheep. Its horns are curly and knobbly.

Antlers

Animals of the deer family have antlers. They are bony, branch-like growths that stick out from the top of the animal's skull. Antlers are shed – that means they fall off – every year. When they are growing, they are covered with soft, fuzzy hair called velvet.

White tailed deer antler

Fox's tooth

Horse's tooth

Deer's tooth

Squirrel's tooth

Teeth

Animal teeth are amazing. They often look very different to human teeth and have evolved to do different jobs.

Did you know?

The longest recorded rhinoceros horn was 1.5 metres.

This is a skeleton

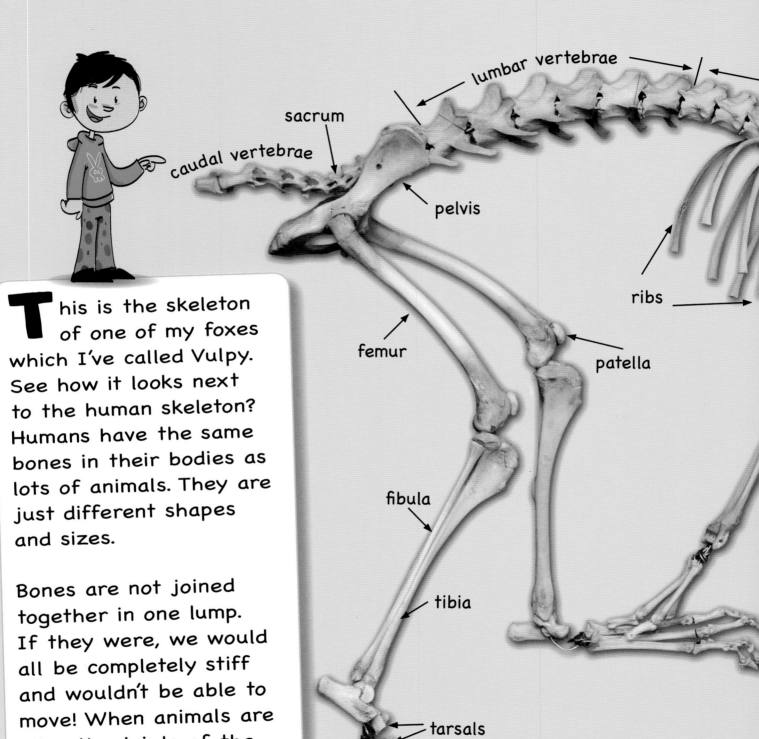

This is the skeleton of one of my foxes which I've called Vulpy. See how it looks next to the human skeleton? Humans have the same bones in their bodies as lots of animals. They are just different shapes and sizes.

Bones are not joined together in one lump. If they were, we would all be completely stiff and wouldn't be able to move! When animals are alive the joints of the skeleton have cartilage in between them.

caudal vertebrae

sacrum

lumbar vertebrae

pelvis

ribs

femur

patella

fibula

tibia

tarsals

metatarsals

phalanges

These are some of the main bones in an animal's body. Bones have quite strange names. This is because we use the names given by the Greeks, Romans and Saxons. Look out for some of the meanings of these names in the book.

cranium

skull: comprises the cranium and mandible (or lower jaw).

cervical vertebrae

thoracic vertebrae

atlas

axis

mandible

scapula

Brilliant Bones

Another name for the humerus (Latin for upper arm) is the funny bone (because it's 'humorous', or funny). When you bang your funny bone it feels strange because it makes a nerve tingle.

humerus

ulna

radius

tarsals would go here

metacarpals

carpals

phalanges

Did you know?

About one fifth of an animal's weight is its skeleton. That means animals – and humans – are 20 per cent bone.

Look! This is a human skeleton. See how we have the same bones as the fox, and most other mammals too.

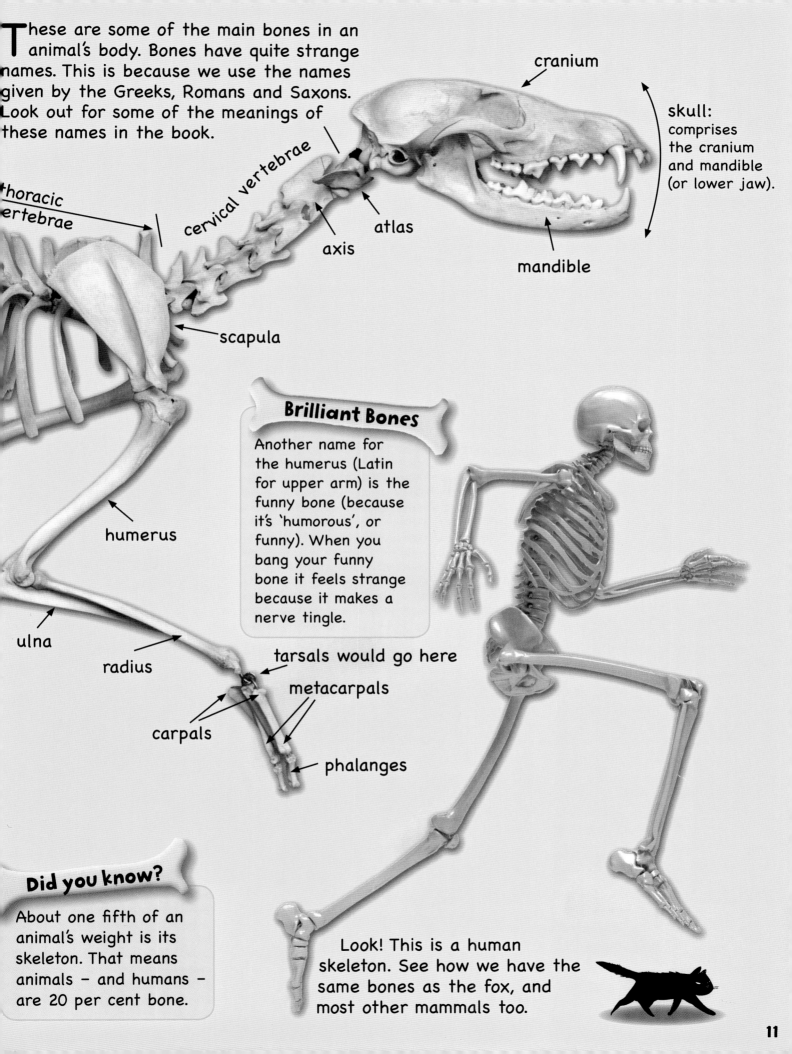

How to recognise a bone

Bones are easy to recognise when you see them as part of a skeleton, but they look very different if you find one on its own. Here are some of the most common bones you might find, and some rarer ones...

Different animals have slightly different bone shapes but you can recognise most mammal bones from the ones on this page. These are all from a roe buck skeleton.

This is what a young roe buck (male deer) looks like.

This skeleton was nearly complete when I found it, but bones quickly get scattered by other creatures that take them away to gnaw.

Vertebrae, or backbones

Every individual backbone is different, but there are four main types: neck, upper back, lower back and tail.

This is the atlas bone – the very top bone of the spine.

This is the axis bone – it's this bone that forms a pivot for the atlas bone so animals and humans can turn their heads.

This is a neck bone.

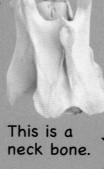

This is an upper backbone.

This is a lower backbone.

This is a tail bone.

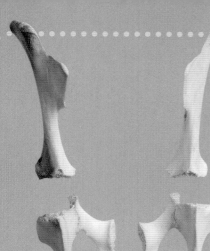

Pelvis

In young animals the pelvis is in four parts.

When animals become adults the cracks in the centre here fuse together so the pelvis is in two parts.

In old animals they fuse down the middle, so the pelvis is in one part.

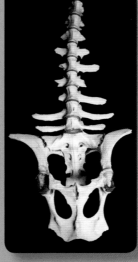

This is a cow's pelvis. See how the bones fit together?

Leg bones

This is a femur, or thigh bone.

These are the patellas, or kneecaps. You don't often find these because they don't connect to any other bone. Put your hand on your knee. Can you feel yours?

This is a tibia, or shin bone. The wide flattish bit is the top, and forms part of the knee joint.

This is the ankle end.

Brilliant Bones

This is the talus, or ankle bone. This one comes from a roe deer. The old game of Knucklebones, or Jacks, used to be played with five sheep ankle bones. They are very tough bones and survive a long time.

Skulls

Every animal skull is different. Sometimes it's easy to see what kind of animal it is and sometimes it's really hard. Here are some of my best and most interesting skulls. I've grouped them into types.

Gnawers

The front teeth, or incisors, of these small animals never stop growing. The orange colour is the enamel, the hard stuff that covers mammal teeth.

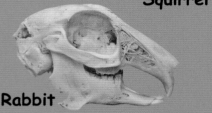

Squirrel

Rabbit

Carnivores

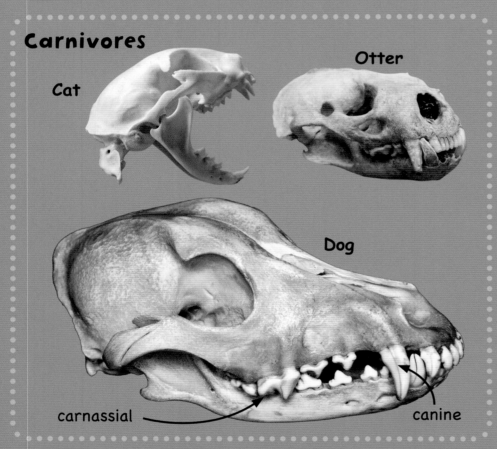

Cat

Otter

Dog

carnassial

canine

Insectivores

Frog

Hedgehog

Armadillo

Different teeth do different jobs
- Incisors bite and cut.
- Canines pierce and tear.
- Pre-molars and molars grind and chew.
- Carnassials shear like scissors.

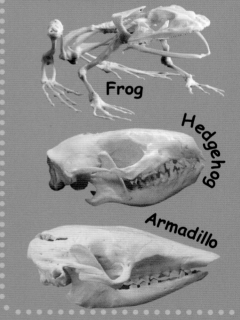

Look at its large pointy teeth.

This is a monkey jaw.

Grazers

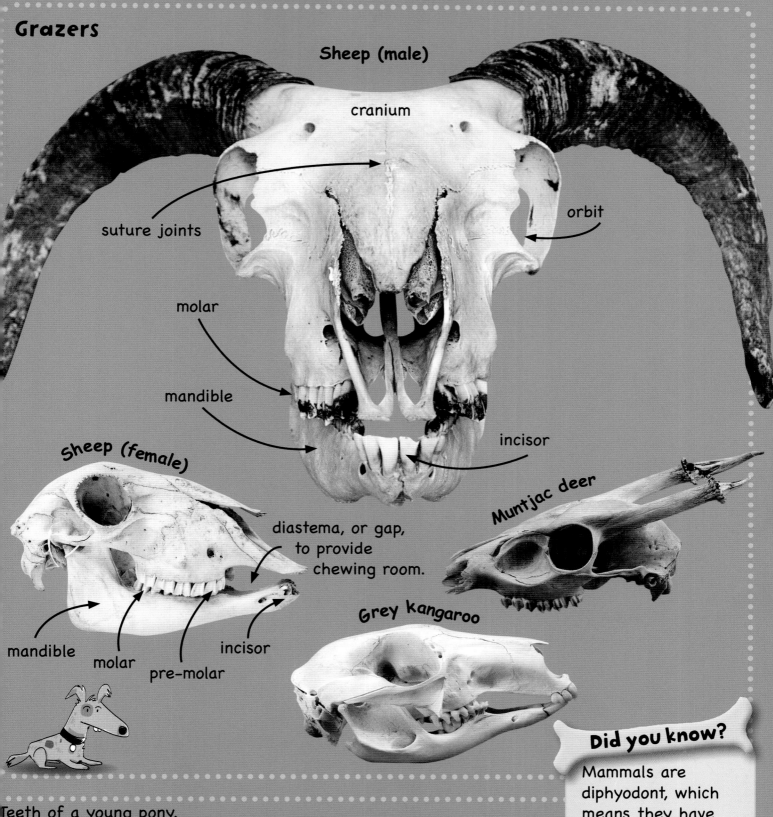

Sheep (male)

cranium

suture joints

orbit

molar

mandible

incisor

Sheep (female)

diastema, or gap, to provide chewing room.

Muntjac deer

mandible

molar

pre-molar

incisor

Grey kangaroo

Teeth of a young pony.

The teeth are just coming through.

This top tooth is old and worn. You can tell because it has big dark patches. The newer teeth below have small dark patches.

Did you know?

Mammals are diphyodont, which means they have two sets of teeth in their lifetime. Deciduous teeth are baby teeth, also called milk teeth. They fall out, just like leaves fall from deciduous trees.

My bone collecting kit

Whenever I go walking in woods, on moors and across fields, these are the things I take with me so I can collect and bring home any bones I find.

Map for the walk and to help log the location of bone finds.

Plastic gloves for touching dirty things.

Marker pen and labels.

A trowel for scraping away soil.

Tape measure to show scale.

Bone Detective

In many countries if you collect a skull of a protected animal you must be able to prove it died of natural causes. This buzzard has a broken neck. It was probably attacked in the sky by crows. The photo helps prove it was a natural death.

Camera to photograph the bones in position.

String to link vertebrae in the right order.

Plastic bags for bone finds.

Bin liners for bigger bone finds.

notebook write any portant details and log where the bones are found.

Old brush (to brush away soil).

Hand wipes and hand gel to clean your hands.

Fox

This is my fox skeleton, Vulpy. It was given to me as a present by a gamekeeper in my village.

There were about 170 bones in total. When I laid them out it looked like this. Almost all the bones are here – even the tiny ones from the feet and tail.

Phalanges – say fal-anjes – are the small bones of the feet. The word comes from the Greek word phalanx, meaning rows of soldiers. The bones of the feet are in rows.

Some of the tail bones are missing.

Foxes live in the country and in towns. They eat everything from birds and frogs to food from rubbish bins.

The lower parts of the back legs are made up of two bones.

tibia

fibula

These are the bones of the paw. The claw sheaths would go over the end bit of bone.

The fibula is mostly used to support muscles and is not very strong.

Bone Detective

Vulpy was a young fox. This is how I can tell: baby mammals are born with more bones in their body than adults. As mammals grow up some of their bones fuse together where they touch to make one bigger bone.

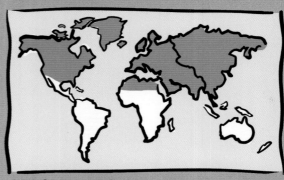

Red foxes are found almost everywhere in the northern half of the world.

The atlas is the first bone in the spine, next to the skull. This bone is named after the mythical Greek god Atlas, who supported the globe of the world.

The atlas bone holds up the 'globe' of the skull. I have put the atlas upside down here, by mistake!

The shoulder blades are called scapulas.

This is how Vulpy's skeleton would look when she was running.

This is Vulpy's skull.

Fox teeth are very much like dog teeth.

Did you know?

Huge cow scapulas were used as shovels in prehistoric times.

Crocodile and Alligator

I got these skulls as presents from two different friends. One is an alligator and still has skin on it, the other is a crocodile. Both are very young and small. The alligator head is 12cm long and the crocodile is 9.5cm long.

You can tell the difference between them by the shape of the skull.

Crocodiles have a long thin v-shaped snout.

Alligators have a wide u-shaped snout.

There is another way you can tell crocodiles and alligators apart. Crocodile teeth fit in between each other and point out a bit.

Look! the tee

Alligator teeth are different because their bottom jaw is smaller than their top jaw, so the bottom teeth sit inside the top teeth when their mouth is shut.

This is a crocodile showing its teeth!

Alligators **A** live in the Southeastern United States and China. Crocodiles **C** live in North and South America, Africa, India, Malaysia and Australia

And here is an alligator from Florida.

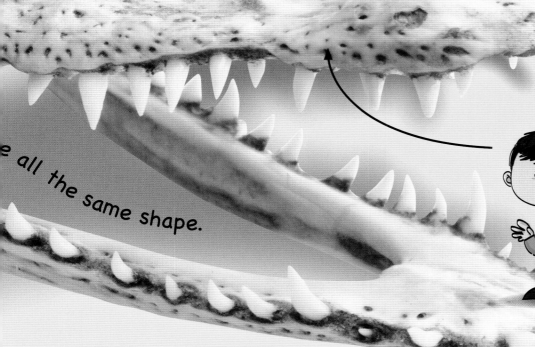

e all the same shape.

There are tiny pits along the jaws. Scientists think these pits are where there are sensors to detect things in the water around them.

Bone Fact

Most mammals, like dogs, cats and humans, have teeth of different shapes to do different jobs. Crocodile and alligator teeth are all the same shape. They are 'homodonts' which means 'same teeth.'

How do animals become bones?

Nature is very tidy. When an animal dies its body breaks down pretty quickly. Bones are the last part of the animal to survive. In warm or hot weather, a deer that died naturally in a wood would take only two to four weeks to become a skeleton. There are lots of different ways this happens...

All animals have their own self destruct mechanism – enzymes and bacteria in their guts. When we are alive enzymes are the chemical reaction machines inside our cells. When we die the enzymes keep on working, breaking down and destroying tissues, with help from the bacteria that help us digest our food.

This is an elephant. Elephants often return to the place where another elephant has died to turn the bones over. We don't know why.

Bone Fact

Rats often gnaw bones and feed on dead animals (also know as carrion). And there's even the mboco, or ivory-eating squirrel, that gnaws bones and tusks of dead elephants!

Flies can sense a newly-dead body in minutes from one mile away. They zoom in and lay eggs on the body. Maggots hatch in a few hours and feed on the body while it's still juicy. When the flesh gets dry, beetle larvae take over. Then mites and millipedes come in.

Flies can fly at 6mph, twice as fast as a human walks.

These are dermestid beetles and their larvae. They eat flesh from bodies, but leave the bones and cartilage without any damage. Bone collectors and museums use them to clean specimens!

Creatures that die in water are food for all sorts of fish and water creatures. Sometimes the bones are washed on the shore by the tide.

Very dry places like deserts can turn animals into mummies. It can take many years for them to become just bones.

It takes longer for animals to become bones in cold places, as insects are less active in the cold.

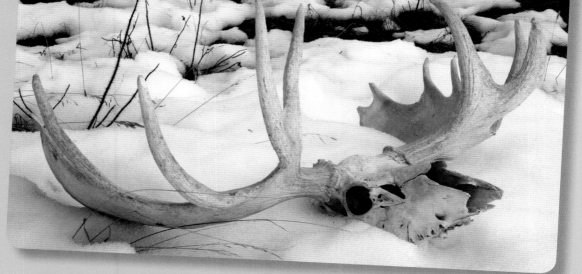

Whale

Whales are sea mammals. There are lots of different types including the blue whale, the biggest creature alive on the planet today. At 30 metres long and 170 tonnes, they are as long as the biggest dinosaurs were and more than twice their weight.

Sometimes a dead whale gets washed up on a beach. When all the bones are clean, the local people put its skeleton back together with bolts and wires and put it up on poles as a tourist attraction.

This is a trick photo. This whale skeleton is on the beach at Fuerteventura, Spain

In the past, whales were hunted almost to extinction. They were used for meat, oil and also for big sheets of keratin in their mouths called baleen plates — filters used to gather the huge amounts of krill whales live on.

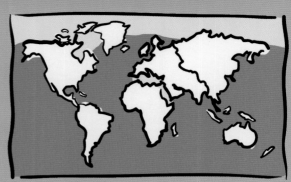

Whales live in oceans all over the world. They swim in polar waters in summer and move nearer the Equator in winter.

baleen plates

he poles have been removed!

Brilliant Bones

Baleen plates are light, strong and flexible. They can even be heated and moulded like plastic.
They were sold to make:
• Ladies skirt frames
• Ladies corsets
• Umbrella spokes
• Military hat frames
• Samurai sword handles
• Carriage springs
• Bed stuffing

George is a roe deer skeleton I found in the wood behind the Roman Fort in my village. The bones were scattered about and some were covered in green algae because they had lain on the ground for months. We found all the big bones, but not many of the little ones like the toes.

The roe deer is a medium sized deer, with a shoulder height of around 70cm. There are lots of species of deer in the world, from the tiny 35cm northern pudú from Ecuador to the 200cm moose.

This is George's skull. George had little stubby antlers, rather than proper antlers.

Bone Detective

George had all his teeth, which means he was not a baby. The third pre-molar on the bottom jaw is an important tooth. When deer are born, their third pre-molar is a baby tooth and has three cusps, or spikes, at the top. George's tooth has two spikes. Roe deer only get this tooth when they are about a year or 13 months old.

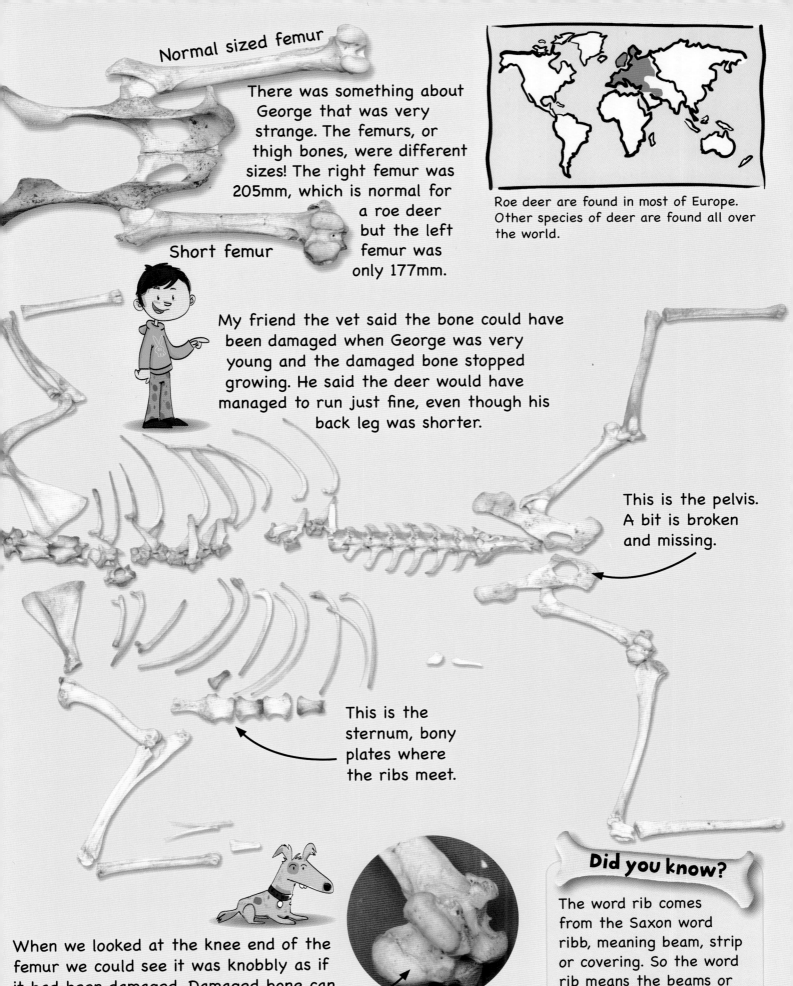

Normal sized femur

There was something about George that was very strange. The femurs, or thigh bones, were different sizes! The right femur was 205mm, which is normal for a roe deer but the left femur was only 177mm.

Short femur

Roe deer are found in most of Europe. Other species of deer are found all over the world.

My friend the vet said the bone could have been damaged when George was very young and the damaged bone stopped growing. He said the deer would have managed to run just fine, even though his back leg was shorter.

This is the pelvis. A bit is broken and missing.

This is the sternum, bony plates where the ribs meet.

When we looked at the knee end of the femur we could see it was knobbly as if it had been damaged. Damaged bone can mend itself, but not always perfectly.

Did you know?

The word rib comes from the Saxon word ribb, meaning beam, strip or covering. So the word rib means the beams or covering of the chest.

How old was the animal?

A bone detective needs to know how an animal grows to be able to work out its age from bones. There are lots of things that tell you whether the animal was old or young when it died – here's what to look for...

Adult deer

Young deer

Baby deer

Shape
Bones change shape when they grow. A young animal has a short nose and big eyes, and an adult animal might have a long nose and smaller eyes. This makes their skulls look different.

Mammals have lines on their skulls called sutures where the skull sections meet. These fuse and become fuzzy or disappear with age.

Fusion
When an animal is young it has lots of bones that will grow together and fuse together as it gets older.

In an adult, all the bones are fused, so adults have bigger bones, but fewer of them.

Teeth
You can also use teeth to find out if an animal is old, as teeth grow and then get worn down during its life.

Deer at birth

First molar

Second molar

Third molar

All adult teeth

Young mammals also have different teeth to grown-up animals – and fewer of them. These are called milk teeth and they get pushed out by the adult teeth that grow from underneath them.

Baby deer pelvis – not fused, four parts.

Adult deer pelvis – fused, one part.

Size

Older animals have bones that look thicker and tougher than the bones of younger animals, with marks on them from where the muscles attached.

Young bone

end not fused

Adult bone

Brilliant Bones

Human babies have up to 350 bones, but human adults only have around 206.

Leopard

One of my favourite skulls is also one of the oldest in my collection. It was sent to me by someone who found my website and it came with lots of other interesting skulls from around the world (see Monkey and Snake). It was also a bit of a mystery skull...

Leopard

I knew straight away it was a big cat because of the shape of the skull, which is just like my cat skull, and because it only had three cheek teeth.

Big cats, like tigers, lions, jaguars and leopards, are really just big versions of my pet cats.

If you watch them at the zoo or on TV, they walk like big pussycats too.

Domestic cat

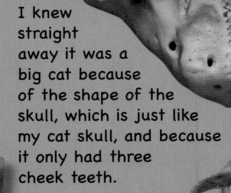

Bone Detective

Every skeleton tells a story about the animal's life and this leopard skull is very strange. The bottom jaw has the canines missing and the left-hand side is the wrong shape. It looks like it has been broken and rehealed. That meant the leopard couldn't eat meat on the left side of its mouth, which would be tough for a carnivore.

Teeth   No teeth

See where it has rehealed? The bone is thicker.

This is the right side of the jaw. This molar looks like it was impacted – meaning it didn't come through properly – and infected. This leopard would have had terrible toothache.

Leopards live in a range of environments from rainforest to desert areas of Asia, Africa, and Siberia.

Leopards are pretty amazing animals. They can run at 37mph, they can climb trees while carrying a dead body, and they have a beautiful coat.

Bone Detective

Here's a possible story: The young leopard was kicked or charged by its prey. Hunting with its injuries was too hard, so it moved closer to a village to stalk farm animals or pets. It would have been a danger to humans – a possible maneater – so it was shot. The leopard's head was examined medically or it was displayed as a trophy. Of course, we'll never know the answer!

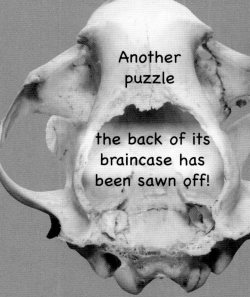

Another puzzle

the back of its braincase has been sawn off!

Snake

This is another skull that was sent to me as a present. It's a snake: a reticulated python; the kind that uses their coils to suffocate their prey. The skull was found in an attic, which must have been a shock for the person who found it!

'Reticulated' means marked like a net. This python has a net-like pattern on its skin.

This snake skull is different to all the other skulls in my collection.

The first big difference is the teeth.

Prey goes one way!

They are sharp as pins and slanted backwards.

There are outer rows and inner rows.

Snakes have a skull, vertebrae and ribs.

Sometimes they have the tiny remains of a pelvis, as snakes' ancestors had legs.

Animal Fact

Snakes swallow their food whole and digest it inside them. They don't chew their food, so don't need cutting teeth like cats or chewing teeth like humans.

The teeth are hooked, a bit like a fishing hook. If this snake bit you, the teeth would go through your skin and it would be difficult to get it off you.

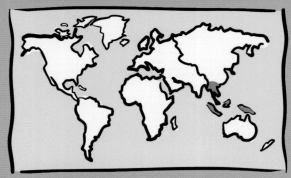

The reticulated python is found in Southeast Asia.

Snakes never stop growing. The record for a reticulated python is over 7.5 metres.

The pelvis is not very easy to see. Look at the kink in the last rib before the tail.

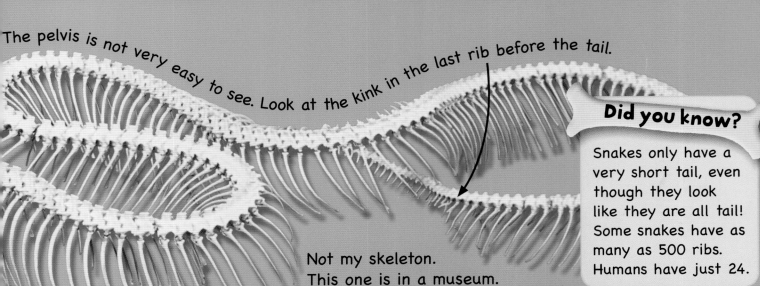

Did you know?

Snakes only have a very short tail, even though they look like they are all tail! Some snakes have as many as 500 ribs. Humans have just 24.

Not my skeleton. This one is in a museum.

Hedgehog

Oscar's feet are missing.

I've called my hedgehog skeleton Oscar. Hedgehogs don't look much like cats, dogs or foxes but their skeletons are surprisingly similar. They even have a tail, though it's hard to see under their spines.

Hedgehogs have around 7,000 25mm-long spines on their backs and sides. These are hollow hairs made of keratin – the same thing human hairs and fingernails are made of.

Hedgehogs have short necks. This is one of the things that makes it easy for them to curl up into a prickly ball when they are in danger.

Did you know?

Hedgehogs can live up to ten years, though they usually only live for three to four years in the wild.

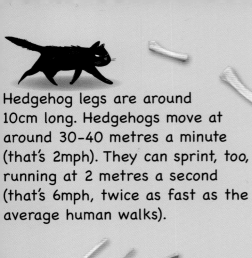

Hedgehog legs are around 10cm long. Hedgehogs move at around 30-40 metres a minute (that's 2mph). They can sprint, too, running at 2 metres a second (that's 6mph, twice as fast as the average human walks).

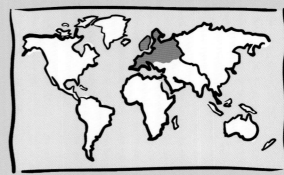

European hedgehogs are found in the western parts of Europe.

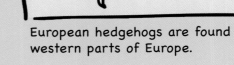

This is the humerus, one of the front leg bones. The top of the humerus isn't joined on, meaning the bone was still growing and the hedgehog was young.

This is Oscar's skull. Hedgehogs are insectivores and live on a diet of beetles, caterpillars, earthworms, bird eggs, slugs and snails. They use their two front teeth to hold their prey.

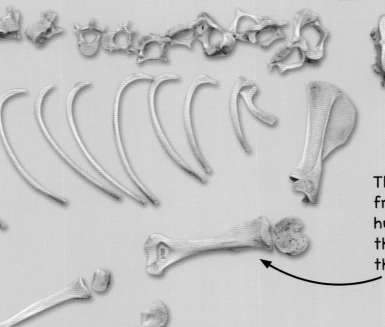

Hedgehogs are cute, but this skull looks like it comes from a savage predator.

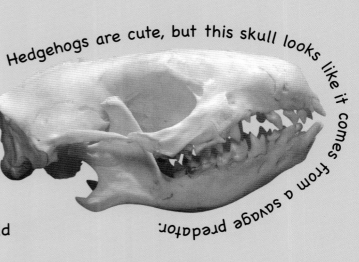

Bird skulls

ird bones are perfectly adapted for flight as they are light and strong. A bird's skeleton weighs less than its feathers!

This is a pigeon skeleton complete with wings. Bird wings are like human arms but with the hands fused together and fewer fingers, plus feathers.

Their beaks are special tools for getting and handling food and have evolved into all sorts of shapes.

Bone Facts

The outer covering of a beak is called a sheath. It is made of keratin – the same stuff as fingernails, hair, horns and feathers. Sheaths are often lost when the bird becomes a skeleton.

Bird bones are hollow with little webs of bone inside to make them strong.

Ducks

Duck and goose skulls are really easy to recognise. They have flat beaks for grazing on grasses and weed and eating small invertebrates and fish.

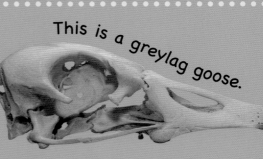

This is a greylag goose.

This is an eider duck.

Eiders live in the sea. They have big beaks with feathers down the sides.

Fish-eating birds

Gannets dive into the water at 60mph to catch fish so their skulls need to be strong.

Did you know?

Puffins have bright orange bits of beak sheath in the breeding season. They fall off when the season ends.

Great black backed gulls swallow food whole or shake it with their beak until it falls apart.

This is a puffin's skull.

This is the world's biggest gull.

Birds of prey

Also called raptors. Their skulls are easy to recognise because of the short beak with a hook at the end, ideal for tearing meat. This golden eagle skull is bigger than a cat's skull! It is the prize of my collection.

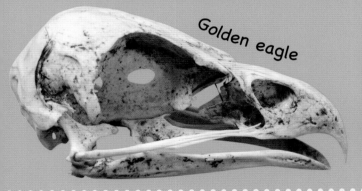

Golden eagle

Kestrel

Buzzard

Unusual beaks

Parrots use their beak for climbing and to tear, crush, crack and peel the nuts, seeds and fruit they eat.

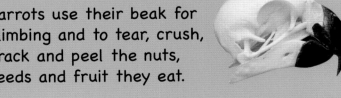

Snipe

The snipe uses its beak as a probe, finding tiny animals to eat in mud and water.

The fulmar is a seabird. Like most seabirds it has salt glands on top of its head. Excess salty water comes out of the glands and through the nostrils. Birds without these glands could die if they drank salt water.

Fulmar

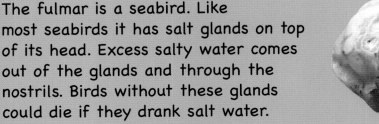

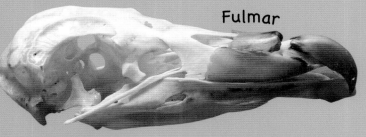

Cat

I have two cats, Bailey, who is black and white, and Eisenstaedt, who is black, so cat skeletons are especially interesting to me. The skeleton below is from a museum and it gives lots of clues as to just how special cats are.

Bailey

Eisenstaedt

Today's domestic cats are descended from the wild cat of Asia and Africa.

The cat's clavicles, or shoulder bones, are not attached to any other bone. They sit inside the shoulder muscles.

This means that cats can pass through gaps as small as their heads without their shoulders getting stuck.

A cat has 30 teeth, including four sharp canines to bite and hold prey.

Their eyes are eight times larger than a human's in relation to head size. They need to be big to let in light for twilight hunting.

Cats have very large eye sockets.

Cat skull

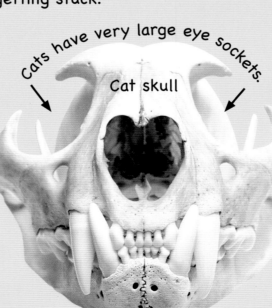

See the small groove where the jawbone joins the skull? This stops the jaw moving from side to side and gives extra power to the animal's bite.

Cats have three more vertebrae than most mammals . . .

. . . this gives their spines extra flexibility.

Domestic cats live all over the world, wherever there are humans.

The vertebrae are also less tightly connected than those of other mammals. This makes it possible for them to arch their backs in a u-shape, and twist their bodies. So they can always land on their feet.

Bone Facts

There are about 240 bones in a cat's body, depending on how many bones they have in their tail. Sometimes they have 18 tail, or caudal, bones, sometimes as many as 28.

Monkey

Monkey skulls are the nearest I have to human skulls in my collection. I have two of different shapes and sizes. They were sent to me as a present together with the leopard on page 30 and the python on page 32.

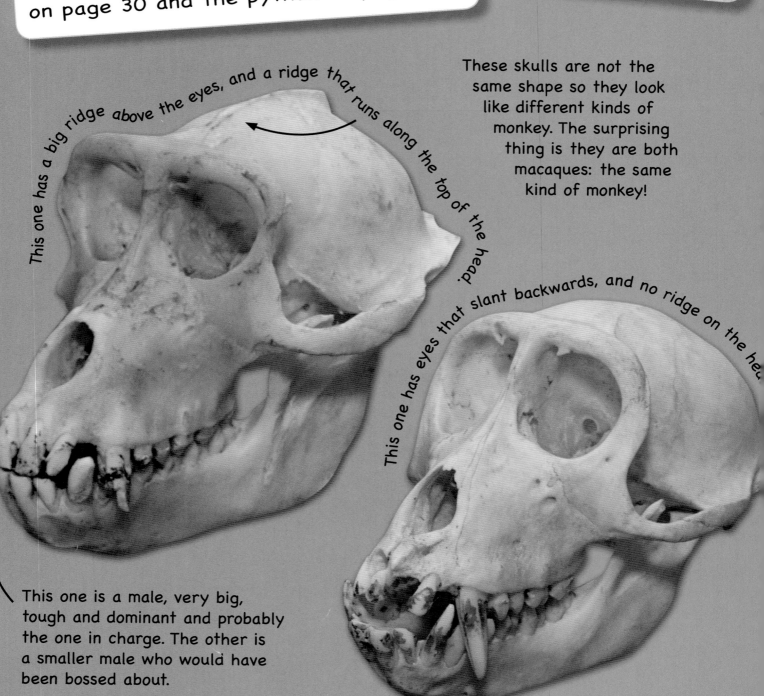

These skulls are not the same shape so they look like different kinds of monkey. The surprising thing is they are both macaques: the same kind of monkey!

This one has a big ridge above the eyes, and a ridge that runs along the top of the head.

This one has eyes that slant backwards, and no ridge on the head.

This one is a male, very big, tough and dominant and probably the one in charge. The other is a smaller male who would have been bossed about.

The back of both skulls is missing.

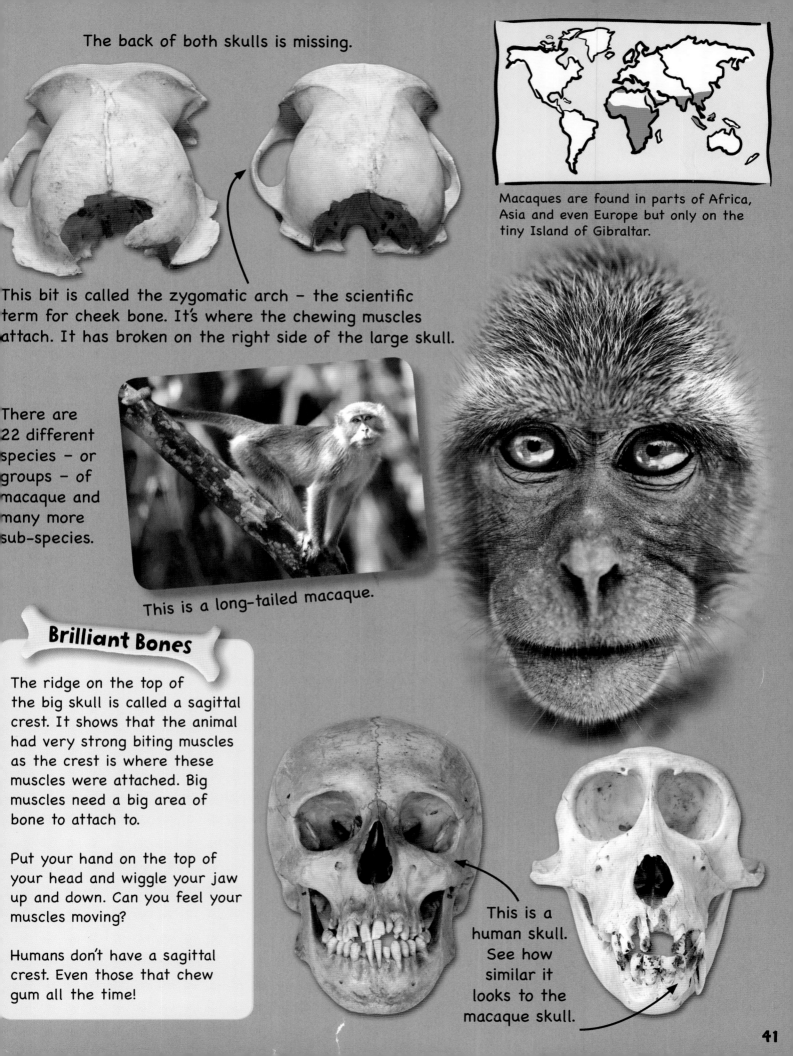

This bit is called the zygomatic arch – the scientific term for cheek bone. It's where the chewing muscles attach. It has broken on the right side of the large skull.

Macaques are found in parts of Africa, Asia and even Europe but only on the tiny Island of Gibraltar.

There are 22 different species – or groups – of macaque and many more sub-species.

This is a long-tailed macaque.

Brilliant Bones

The ridge on the top of the big skull is called a sagittal crest. It shows that the animal had very strong biting muscles as the crest is where these muscles were attached. Big muscles need a big area of bone to attach to.

Put your hand on the top of your head and wiggle your jaw up and down. Can you feel your muscles moving?

Humans don't have a sagittal crest. Even those that chew gum all the time!

This is a human skull. See how similar it looks to the macaque skull.

The biggest bones...

The biggest bone in the world today belongs to the biggest animal – the blue whale, whose jawbone measures around 7 metres from end to end. The smallest mammal jawbone is around 7mm long and belongs to the bumblebee bat. That's a thousand times smaller than the whale jaw. The smallest bone is probably the stirrup bone in the ear of the lightest mammal, the white-toothed pygmy shrew.

This is a sperm whale. They are only two thirds the size of the blue whale. The skull weighs 650kg. My skull weighs 550g. The whale skull weighs more than a thousand skulls like mine!

This blue whale jawbone weighs almost 700kg. That's 20 times as much as I weigh, and 150 times as much as one of my cats.

Animal Fact

An African elephant molar weighs the same as one of my cats.

This Staffordshire terrier is sitting beside an African elephant femur in Zimbabwe. African elephants are the heaviest living land animal. Their femurs measure just over a metre long.

and the smallest

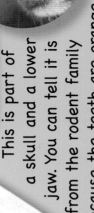

This is the smallest bone I found. It looks like a neck vertebrae. It is only 2.5mm long!

Owls eat their prey whole and spit up the bones and fur in the form of pellets. I found this pellet under trees at the edge of a wood.

I picked one apart with cocktail sticks and tweezers to see what bones were inside.

This is part of a skull and a lower jaw. You can tell it is from the rodent family because the teeth are orange on the front. I think it is a small mouse – maybe a harvest mouse.

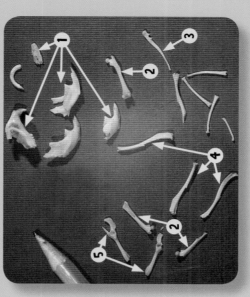

These are all from the same pellet but they came from more than one animal.

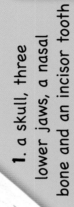

1. a skull, three lower jaws, a nasal bone and an incisor tooth
2. three femurs
3. an ulna, which is one of the front lower leg bones
4. tibia, or shin bones
5. pelvis bones

Here's another one I picked apart. You can see:
1. four halves of a pelvis
2. five radiuses, one ulna
3. three femurs
4. and four tibia
. . . so the owl must have eaten at least three mouse-sized mammals!

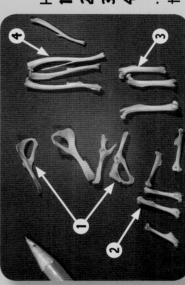

Bones on the beach

Beaches are really good places to find bones, especially if they don't get many human visitors. All sorts of things get washed up on the shore, from fish to mammals to seabirds. Sometimes they are land animals but more often they have come from the sea.

This is a pig skull. I wonder how it came to be washed up on the beach?

These are cow bones.

They have been washed smooth by the sea.

sacrum

rib

rib

This is a skeleton of a Cape fur seal. These seals live on the coast of Australia, Angola, Gabon, Mozambique, Namibia and South Africa.

vertebrae

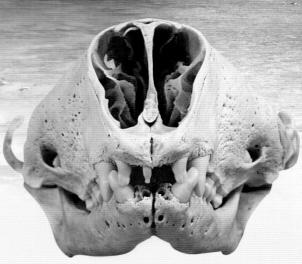

You can find all sorts of bones on beaches, especially fish bones. Take a look at my monkfish over the page.

The skull is big – about 25cm long

This is the most amazing beach find. It was discovered by a friend in Northumberland in England. It's chunky, rough and solid and it looks like some kind of savage animal, but it's a grey seal!

Seals can live up to 25–35 years, but the teeth on this one seem very sharp, so I think it was an adult but not that old.

These are seals lounging on some rocks in Scotland.

Animal Fact

The Latin name for a grey seal is *Halichoerus grypus* which means 'hook-nosed sea pig'.

Monkfish

This skull was sent to me by a bone collector I sometimes swap skulls with. He didn't tell me what it was but I guessed it was some kind of fish – and I was right! It's a monkfish, probably *Lophius piscatorius*. Monkfish are also called goosefish or anglerfish. Females 'fish' for prey with a rod that comes out of their forehead.

The first thing you notice about this skull are the thin spiky teeth. I counted 97!

The bottom jaw has two rows – small spikes in front that point upwards, then bigger spikes that curve back into the mouth.

The fish had even more teeth than this skull shows! The skull is missing a bony plate inside its mouth that also has teeth on it.

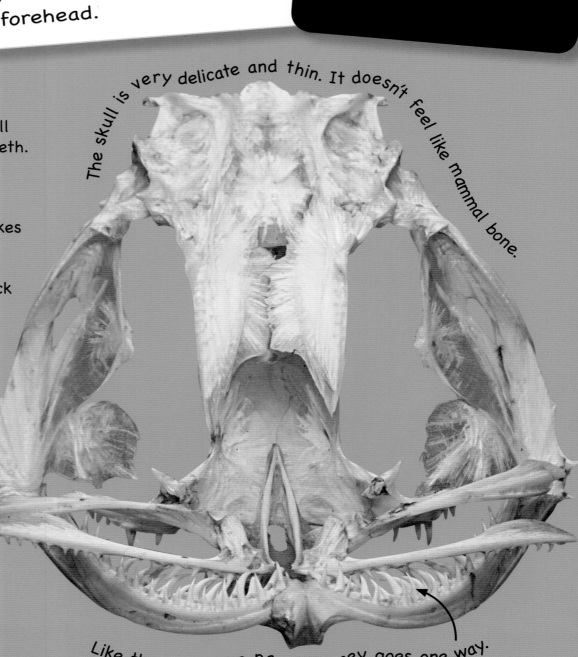

The skull is very delicate and thin. It doesn't feel like mammal bone.

Like the python on page 32, prey goes one way.

46

Brilliant Bones

Monkfish mouths are huge and their skin and skeletons are so flexible that they can swallow prey as big as themselves.

The hardest part is the forehead that protects the braincase. Even so it feels like you could put your finger through it.

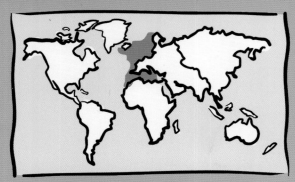

Monkfish live in both deep and shallow waters in the seas around Europe from Iceland to the Mediterranean. Other species live along the African coast and in the Atlantic Ocean.

Look at the ridges and spikes.

The braincase is absolutely tiny so it must have had a very small brain.

This is the back view.

Bone Fact

Monkfish are classified as bony fish, which means their bones are made of the same stuff as mammal bones. Not all fish have bones like this. Sharks are cartilaginous, which means their skeleton is made of cartilage – the stuff mammals have between their bones.

Many monkfish live in the deep ocean where there is no light, so their lure has a luminous tip powered by bioluminescent bacteria. When other fish come to investigate the light they get swallowed.

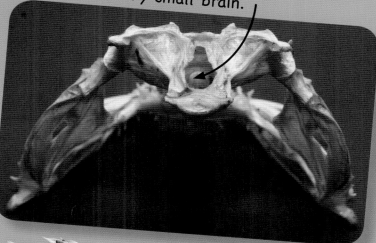

Unusual bones

Lots of the fun of bone collecting is in finding out new things, and especially finding bones that are really strange. Here are some of my best bone discoveries.

The furcula strengthens the pectoral girdle (all of the chest area) and makes it easier for the bird to fly, by acting like a spring when it's flapping.

The first time I found this type of bone I didn't know what it was. I kept it because it was unusual. It's called a furcula. Birds have it, and dinosaurs had it, too.

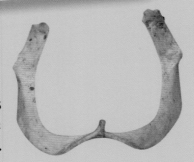

Millions of years ago, it used to be two different bones, the collarbones, which have joined together over time.

You might recognise it from your dinner. It's also called a wishbone. This one's from a chicken.

Sometimes ordinary bones look really strange.

humerus

radius   ulna

This is the normal leg, from Alice, my deer.

This is the leg of Francis, a badly injured red deer.

Three broken bones have healed together.

The bones are lighter than they were before because the deer didn't put weight on it after it broke. Most animals can manage fine on three legs.

Bone Detective

Here's what I think happened: Francis broke his or her leg and it didn't heal properly. It probably took up to a year to mend. Francis was good at hiding in the woods and died naturally.

found this bone in a place called Duck Skull Valley.

It's not very big, and it feels smoother and thinner than most bones.

It came from the skeleton of a duck, and it took two museum experts to help me identify it.

They told me it's a duck syrinx (say sihr-inks). It comes from the duck's windpipe, which is the tube from the throat to the lungs. The cool bit is that this is the bit that makes the duck's quacking noise!

The duck it came from was a mallard, like this one.

Did you know?

That some very unusually small human bones have led scientists to announce a new species of humans that existed 12,000 years ago. The bones, found in a cave on an island near Indonesia in 2004, indicate that these people were all under 1 metre tall! They have called the new species *Homo floresiensis* but nicknamed them 'Hobbit' people.

Moles spend most of their life below the ground digging, so they need very strong upper arms. A mole's humerus (upper arm bone) is hardly recognisable because it is so specially adapted. It is much wider and shorter than other animals' humeri, with lots of space for muscle attachments at the shoulder.

Dinosaur bones

Some bones last for millions of years after the animal has died. This is how we know about dinosaurs, creatures that lived on Earth between 230 and 65 million years ago. Dinosaur remains are found all over the world. They are some of the most exciting bones of all time.

There are three kinds of evidence for dinosaurs:

1 Fossils where bones, flesh, skin, guts, scales, eggs and even feathers get replaced by minerals that preserve them.

This looks a bit like a Tyrannosaurus re.

Mostly fossils are buried under the ground. They can be exposed as cliffs are eroded by the sea, as they are dug out of quarries or sometimes even out of people's gardens.

2 Impressions where the animal's body dissolves away, but leaves a detailed outline in special kinds of rock.

3 Trace fossils where footprints or burrows have been filled with sediment and become rock. These show where dinosaurs walked or lived.

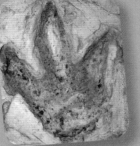

Some dinosaurs are still alive today. Birds are a very successful group of meat-eating dinosaurs that evolved flight around 150 million years ago.

...t it's actually a Carnotaurus, which means 'meat-eating bull'. Look at the horn.

Bone Detective

In 2009 a four-year-old girl called Daisy found a strange black bone sticking out of the sand on the Isle of Wight, England. It turned out to be a new species of pterosaur, or flying reptile. Scientists have named it after her: *Vectidraco daisymorrisae*.

Triceratops

The *Triceratops* has one of the greatest skulls ever, with three horns and a huge bony frill. Lots of Triceratops bones have been found in Asia, Alaska, western Canada and western America, including complete skeletons.

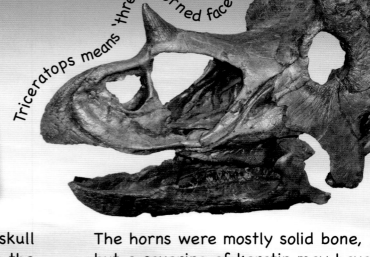

Triceratops means 'three-horned face'.

Triceratops lived 65-63 million years ago. Its skull made up a third of its total body length. It is the largest skull of all land animals ever to have lived.

The horns were mostly solid bone, but a covering of keratin may have made them twice as long.

Nobody knows why the *Triceratops* skull has a frill and horns, but scientists now think it was partly for defence but also for display, so they could identify each other and impress each other during courtship. So they were probably just big show-offs.

This is an artist's impression of *Triceratops'* markings. Some palaeontologists think that their skin might have been covered in bristles.

Bone Detective

The big meat-eating *T. rex* preyed on Triceratops. Scratches on fossil skulls match *T. rex* tooth marks and scientists think that *T. rex* pulled the *Triceratops'* head off to make it easier to eat.

Museums all over the world have *Triceratops* skulls on display.

Triceratops reconstructions are really cool. This one shows how big they grew.

T. rex

T.rex bones have been found in Montana, South Dakota, Wyoming, Colorado and Texas in America and Alberta in Canada. None of them were complete skeletons. We know what the dinosaur looked like by comparing all the bone finds.

The dinosaur bones you see in museums are made out of resin.

This is a T. rex vertebrae. The scientist is preparing a mould for casting out of toy bricks.

This is a model T. rex and the skeleton next to it is about the same size as my dad.

Tyrannosaurus means 'tyrant lizard'.

T. rex's arms may look tiny but they were still 1 metre long.

No one knows why their arms were so small, but they were probably useful for getting up again if they fell over.

I saw this T. rex skull in the Gallery of Palaeontology and Comparative Anatomy in Paris.

T. rex probably had about 200 bones. Adult humans have around 206. T. rex's jaws were up to 1.2 metres long.

It had 50 to 60 huge teeth.

T. rex sometimes ate the bones of the animals it hunted. We know this because crushed bones were found in its dung.

T. rex walked on three clawed toes. It had a smaller toe on its leg like a bird. This is called a hallux.

Digging up dinosaurs

Palaeontologists are people who discover and study dinosaur bones. They need to know about geology (the study of the Earth) as well as biology (the study of living organisms). The bones they find help us understand the past and often the bones go on display in museums.

This palaeontologist is a mountain climber, too. He is digging a *Centrosaurus* toe bone from a cliff in Dinosaur Provincial Park, Canada. Forty species of dinosaur have been discovered in this area.

These palaeontologists are working on an almost vertical quarry face called 'Dinosaur Wall' in Dinosaur National Monument on the border of Colorado and Utah in America.

When rock was removed from the quarry, hundreds of Late Jurassic dinosaur bones were discovered. The bones are 150 million years old.

The rock contains remains of meat-eating *Allosaurus*, the great plant-eating sauropod *Camarasaurus lentus*, and *Stegosaurus*.

Just as anyone can find animal bones, anyone can discover dinosaur bones. In 1980, schoolboy Jeff Baker was on a fishing trip in Alberta, Canada, when he saw a bone poking out of a river bank. It was part of a *T. rex* skeleton that would become known by the nickname of Black Beauty because of its black shiny bones.

It is the smallest and one of the most complete *T. rex* skeletons ever found and is in the Royal Tyrrell Museum in Alberta.

Models of Black Beauty are on display all over the world. This model is being welded together for a travelling show.

Here is a *Stegosaurus*

These dinosaurs probably died in lots of different floods over many years and their bodies were trapped in mud that later hardened into rock.

Brilliant Bones

Lots of people study bones. They are all called different things.

- Archaeologists study the human past – dead people, the places they lived and their stuff.
- Archaeozoologists and Zooarchaeologists study animal remains on archaeological sites.
- Palaeontologists study prehistoric life.
- Zoologists study all animals, living and extinct.

Any of these experts might also be a Curator - someone who looks after collections of things in museums.

These experts all love the particular thing that they do and don't like it if you muddle their jobs and their job titles up!

Your bone collection

Anyone can start a bone collection and you never know where collecting might take you. Perhaps you might be the one to find a fact-changing bone! Here are my tips on how to make your collection the best it can be.

I keep my bones in plastic boxes. It holds all the bits together and keeps them free from dust.

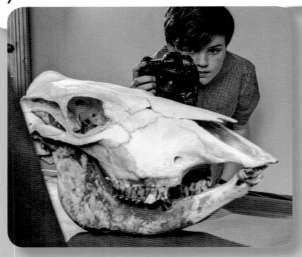

Use a scale

When you photograph your bones, a scale – an object that everyone recognises the size of – helps to show how big they are. A pencil works well.

This is a newt skeleton. It's tiny!

Take photographs

Put your bones on a plain coloured background. I chose red for my blog and orange, yellow, green and blue for my book.

Tag it

All the bones in your collection need a label so they don't get muddled up.

Femur
Roe deer
9105

On one side Write:
- Animal bone
- Animal name
- Special number

On the other side write:
- Date collected
- Place collected
- Person who collected it/gave it to you
- How it was collected

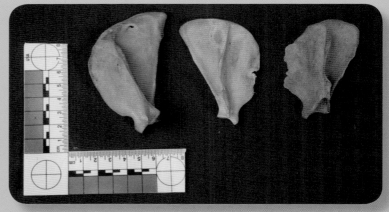

This is a scientific scale marked in centimetres and millimetres. You can download scales from the internet and print them out.

If you're out and about you can use your foot. It's not properly scientific, but it works.

Catalogue it

The special number on the tag is useful for making a catalogue. All the experts do this: museum curators, archaeologists, palaeontologists and grown-up collectors.

I use yellow paper for bones I found myself, pink for gifts and blue for bones I bought. I put a photo on each page and add the details and the number on the label.

You can do this on a computer, or you can write it out by hand. Make sure you use a permanent pen! Biro fades after a few years.

JAKE'S BONES	Specimen Record	Number 2499
		Kept Bedroom top shelf
		Acquired 10/11/2012
		Found myself Titus Well Wood
Specimen	Red deer	Licence No. None needed
Type	Skull	
Details	Juvenile red deer stag skull, between 1 and 2 years (M2 emerged but no M3) found discarded by gamekeeper on track at Titus Well Wood	

This is my template. Each skull or skeleton gets its own page.

Almost all museum collections started out as the collections of individual people.

These skeletons are in the Gallery of Palaeontology and Comparative Anatomy in the Natural History Museum in Paris.

This is a picture of Barnum Brown taken in 1934. He collected fossils and bones as a boy. He grew up to become the chief fossil hunter for the American Museum of Natural History in New York.

Brilliant Bones

There's a biologist and bone collector in San Francisco who has 7,000 skulls – his name is Ray Bandar and he started collecting when he was a boy like me.

Seven golden rules

The brilliant thing about collections is that you can't plan what's going to go in it. You never know what you might find and that turns collecting into an adventure. But all adventures mean care and responsibility. Here are my golden rules for safe, legal and sustainable bone collecting:

1 Do no harm

No animal should come to harm for the sake of your collection. This is the first rule and the most important one of all (and make sure you keep yourself safe, too).

2 Make sure your bone collection is legal

CITES stands for Convention on International Trade in Endangered Species of Wild Fauna and Flora. It is an international agreement between governments. Its aim is to make sure that international trade in specimens of wild animals and plants does not threaten their survival. Always check their website (on page 64) before buying a new bone or skull. Each country has its own laws, too.

It is illegal to buy sea turtle bones.

3 Be considerate

Close gates, don't go bone hunting on private land without permission and always tell a grown up where you're going. Handle bones carefully.

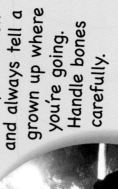

This is a brown hare.

5 Treat your collection with respect

Remember that the bones once belonged to living creatures.

4 Nature needs bones too

Only take as many bones as you need, as nature needs bones more than you do. Lots of animals like to gnaw bones. They help keep rodent teeth short and also provide many animals with calcium.

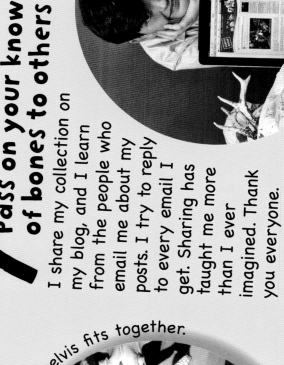

7 Pass on your knowledge of bones to others

I share my collection on my blog, and I learn from the people who email me about my posts. I try to reply to every email I get. Sharing has taught me more than I ever imagined. Thank you everyone.

6 Let bones from dead animals teach you about living nature

This is how Vulpy the fox's pelvis fits together.

Studying bones helps you to understand how animals live and how their bodies – and our bodies – work.

Glossary

ALGAE – tiny organisms that get energy from light

ANTLER – a bony branching structure that deer fight with

ARCHAEOLOGIST – someone who studies humans from the past

ARCHAEOZOOLOGIST – someone who studies animals used by humans in the past

ATLAS – neck bone that supports the skull, named after a Greek god

AXIS – neck bone that the atlas sits on and which lets the skull turn

BACTERIA – simple organisms that you need a microscope to see

BALEEN – food filters used by whales, made out of keratin

BIOLOGIST – someone who studies living things

BIOLUMINESCENT – living organisms that glow

BONE MARROW – tissue that makes blood cells

BRAINCASE – the part of the skull that holds the brain

BUCK – a male deer

CALCIUM SALTS – minerals containing calcium that are important in biology

CANINES – pointy teeth used for fighting and killing prey

CARNASSIALS – cutting teeth in a meat-eater

CARNIVORE – a meat-eater

CARPALS – bones of the hand

CARRION – dead animals

CARTILAGE – flexible, rubbery material that connects bones

CAUDAL VERTEBRAE – tail bones

CELLS – the tiny building blocks that make living things

CERVICAL VERTEBRAE – neck bones

CITES – an international legal agreement that controls the trade in endangered species

CLAVICLES – collarbones

COLLAGEN – a long protein that adds strength to bones, tendons and even skin

COMPACT BONE – dense and strong material on the outside part of bones

CRANIUM – the upper part of the skull

CURATOR – someone who looks after a collection

CUSPS – bumps on teeth to help chewing

DECIDUOUS TEETH – also known as baby or milk teeth. The first set of teeth in a mammal, that are shed when the permanent teeth emerge

DERMESTID BEETLE – a type of beetle that eats dead animals

DIASTEMA – a useful gap in the arrangement of an animal's teeth

DINOSAUR – 'terrible lizards' that went extinct 65 million years ago

DIPHYODONT – animals with two sets of teeth during their lifetime

ENAMEL – the hardest material made by an animal. It covers teeth and makes them strong

ENZYMES – folded proteins that do all sorts of jobs in the body, including breaking down food

ERODED – worn away

EVOLVED – changed over a long time

EXOSKELETON – a hard covering on the outside of an animal that provides support

FEMUR – the thigh bone

FIBULA – a thin bone in the lower leg

FOSSIL – an animal that has been preserved in rock.

FURCULA – a wishbone. The fusion of the furcula.

FUSE – join together

GEOLOGY – the study of rocks and the Earth

HALLUX – a toe sticking out of the back of the foot in a dinosaur or bird

HOMODONT – 'Homo' means same and 'dont' means teeth – so homodont is teeth that look the same

HUMERUS – the upper arm bone

INCISORS – the front teeth

INFECTED – when harmful bacteria grow in something

INORGANIC – molecules that don't contain chains of carbon

INSECTIVORES – things that eat insects and other invertebrates

INVERTEBRATES – animals without a backbone

KERATIN – a strong protein in long chains made by animals

KRILL – a tiny sort of invertebrate that lives in the ocean

LARVAE – the young stage of some animals. For example, maggots are the larvae of flies

LUMBAR VERTEBRAE – backbones from the lower part of the spine

MACAQUE – a widespread type of monkey

MAMMAL – animals with fur that are fed on milk by their mothers

MANDIBLE – the lower jawbone

METACARPALS – bones of the hand

METATARSALS – bones of the foot

MINERALS – solid chemicals

MOLAR – the back teeth, for chewing

MUMMIES – dried out bodies

MUSCLE – living tissue that gets longer and shorter to make bodies move

NASAL BONE – the bones of the nose

ORBIT – the eye socket

ORGANIC – made of chains of carbon atoms

PALAEONTOLOGY – the study of life in the past

PATELLA – the kneecap

PECTORAL GIRDLE – the bones of the chest and shoulders

PELLETS – balls of fur, feathers and bone coughed up by owls and birds of prey

PERMANENT TEETH – also known as adult teeth. The second set of teeth in a mammal, that last for the rest of the animal's life

PELVIS – the bones of the hips

PHALANGES – the bones of the fingers and toes

PRE-MOLARS – the chewing middle teeth

PTEROSAUR – an extinct flying reptile

RADIUS – a bone of the lower arm

RESIN – material used to make detailed casts of bones

RETICULATED – a net-like pattern

RIBS – bone strips in the chest that protect the internal organs

RODENTS – the group of mammals including rats, mice and squirrels

SACRUM – a bone made of fused vertebrae that connects the spine to the pelvis

SAGITTAL CREST – a bony ridge along the top of some skulls, where muscles attach

SALT GLANDS – glands that remove salt from the blood of birds and reptiles

SHEATHS – coverings of keratin over bone

SKELETON – the supporting structure of a body

SKULL – the cranium and mandible

SPONGE-LIKE BONE – light and delicate bony structure with lots of gaps on the inside of some bones

STERNUM – fused bones in the front part of the chest where the ribs join

STIRRUP BONE – a tiny bone inside the ear of mammals

SUTURE – the join between two pieces of bone

SYRINX – an organ that makes sound in birds

TALUS – a bone in the ankle

TARSALS – bones of the lower foot

TENDON – tough tissues that connect muscles to bones

THORACIC VERTEBRAE – bones of the upper part of the back, where the ribs attach

TIBIA – the shinbone

TISSUE – a combination of cells of a similar type

ULNA – a bone in the lower part of the arm or front leg

VELVET – skin with lots of blood vessels that lay down the bone in antlers

VERTEBRAE – bones of the back

ZOOARCHAEOLOGISTS – someone who studies animals used by humans in the past

ZOOLOGIST – someone who studies animals

ZYGOMATIC ARCH – the cheekbone

Index

For more information on legal and safe bone collecting go to **www.cites.org**

• •

Picture Acknowledgements

All photography by Nick McGowan-Lowe, except for the following:

Alamy A & J Visage 33 centre; Andrew Murdoch 14 centre left below; Armand-Photo-Nature 48 below; Chris Parks 32 below; Eddie Gerald 38 centre; FLPA 23 below; J. M. Labat/Visual&Written SL 36 above; James Soden/Bernwood Press 61 above left; Nick Jene 52 above; Norbert Rosing 23 centre left; Paul Carter 59 below left; Roswitha Reisinger 4 below, 24; Sally Anne Thompson/Animal Photography 39 centre; travelpixs 48 above right; WaterFrame 46 above.
Corbis Bettmann 59 below right; Friso Gentsch/dpa 42 above left; Kayte Deioma/ZUMA Press 50 main; Ken Lucas/Visuals Unlimited 57 above left; Louie Psihoyos 51 above right, 54 above, 55 main, 56 above, 56 main, 57 above right; Richard T. Nowitz 42 main.
FLPA Terry Whittaker 29 above right.
Fotolia argot 14 centre right; creativenature.nl 43 above centre; dmitry_saparov 23 centre; natureimmortal 12 above; Omika 34 below; Stéphane Bidouze 41 centre left; Vladislav Gajic 54 centre left.
Getty Images David Cantrell, 3 and 3 Studios 49 above right.
Joanne Bourne 8 below right.
Rex Isle of Wight County Press 51 below centre.
Science Photo Library Patrick Landmann 6; Scientifica, Visuals Unlimited 39 below.
Shutterstock Orla 11 right; Sorbis 21 above right; ragnisphoto 26 above left.
SuperStock age fotostock 47 below; Biosphoto 42 below, 44 above right; Exactostock 8 below centre; Science Photo Library 54 centre; Stocktrek Images 53 above right.
The Bridgeman Art Library Ali Meyer 13 below right. The Horniman Museum and Gardens Paolo Viscardi 49 below left, 49 below right.
Thinkstock 52 main; Brand X Pictures 16 above left; George Doyle 16 below right; Hemera 23 centre right, 39 above, 44 above, 55 below right; Hemera Technologies 17 below centre, 17 below left; iStock 2, 5 above right, 6 below left, 7 above left, 7 above right, 8 centre right, 9 above left, 9 above right, 9 centre, 9 below left, 9 below right, 13 below centre left, 16 centre left, 16 below centre left, 16 below centre, 17 above right, 17 centre right above, 17 centre right, 17 centre right below, 17 below centre right, 17 below right, 18 left, 21 above left, 22, 23 above left, 28–29 centre, 30 centre left, 30 below, 31 centre, 32 above, 34 above, 37 above right, 38 below left, 40 above, 41 centre right, 41 below left, 43 below centre, 44 above left, 48 centre right, 50 above right, 50 below right, 51 above left, 51 above centre, 60 below, 61 below left; Jupiterimages 24 above; Wavebreak Media 16 below left.